KANGAROOS

KANGAROOS

Denise Burt
Photographs by Neil McLeod

J.M. Dent & Sons Ltd
London

First published in Great Britain in 1989
by J.M. Dent & Sons Ltd

Text © Denise Burt 1989
Photographs © Neil McLeod 1989
(Except those separately acknowledged)

Printed in Hong Kong

British Library Cataloguing-in-Publication Data

Burt, Denise
Kangaroos
1. Kangaroos
I. Title
599.2
ISBN 0 460 07051 7

The producer gratefully acknowledges
permission granted by the Commonwealth
Scientific and Industrial Research
Organization, Division of Wildlife and
Ecology, Canberra, Australia, to use the
transparencies for the illustrations on
pages 20, 21, 22 and 23.

Originated and produced by Buttercup Books Pty Ltd
21 McLochlan Street, Mount Waverley, 3149, Victoria,
Australia

Distribution of Red Kangaroos

Distribution of Wallaroos and Euros

Distribution of Grey Kangaroos

Distribution of Swamp Wallaby

In 1912 Alfred Wegener, a German astronomer, proposed a theory that all the continents on earth were once a single land mass, which he called Gondwana, after the Indian people in whose region the first fossil plant was found. This theory is now referred to as the 'continental drift'. When the moving plates of the ocean floor split the great southern continent, South America, Antarctica and Australia were formed. These new continents took with them new species of fauna as well as the original ones. Very early in the break up New Zealand drifted away and the marsupial mammals — animals with a pouch on the lower part of the female's stomach in which she carries her young — which evolved in Australia could not reach New Zealand. Because of their isolation the marsupials in Australia prospered.

The first marsupials were probably small, tree-dwelling possums. As they grew bigger and had to compete for food, they began to come down from the trees. Their digestive systems adapted to the different forms of food and they developed a hindlegged bounding gait, which enabled them to live among the shrubs and ground cover of the early Australian forests. They were able to use their back legs for hopping and their forepaws could easily reach the green shoots for feeding.

When the forests receded and were replaced by grasslands, the marsupials adapted to the coarser grasses on which they grazed and they thrived on the extra nutrients contained in them.

Their hind feet and legs grew longer and more powerful. The tail also grew longer and stronger, giving the kangaroo more balance and acting as a prop while moving slowly or sitting. With this development of the longer hind legs and shorter forelegs, some of the marsupials' climbing ability disappeared but, strangely, some of the kangaroos and wallabies later returned to the trees.

Australia has the greatest number of marsupials in the world and the kangaroo family is the largest of all the marsupials. There are many varieties of kangaroos, all having the same features in common, but different in size, colour, length of paws, tails, ears, etc.

In this book we can only cover some of the two main families — the POTOROIDAE, and the MICROPODIDAE, and have loosely brought them together under the one heading of Kangaroos.

This is a young Swamp Wallaby, which is found along the length of the eastern coastal regions. It likes to shelter in dense grass and ferns and sometimes rests in wet spots on hillsides in open eucalypt forests during the day. It emerges at night on brigalow (Acacia) scrub.

The coarse fur and small body size (only about 29 in — 756 mm) probably protects it from commercial hunters who do not think it worthwile.

This distinctly marked Bridled Nailtail Wallaby has a small horny spur at the end of its tail, rather like a small finger nail, but it serves no useful purpose. It uses its long, strong claws on its forepaws to scrape hollows in which to rest during the day.

The Antilopine Wallaroo is found in the northern parts of Australia and is particularly common in Arnhem Land. This wallaroo is more slender and long limbed than other wallaroos and resembles the Grey and Red Kangaroo in general appearance and behaviour.

It is found in open eucalypt woodlands, mostly on flat or gently undulating land. The head and body length of an adult male is approx. 42 in (1064 mm) and it weighs about 118 lbs (53.6 kg).

This is the large but graceful Red Kangaroo, which inhabits the inland plains where the rainfall may be as low as 15 in (381 mm). The colour of the males has given them the common name, but the female has a bluish colour and is usually called the 'blue flier'.

They have well proportioned bodies with distinctive large ears. An adult male can measure 45 in (1150 mm) from nose to the end of the body, with a tail of 35 in (880 mm), weighing about 66 lb (30 kg). The female's body is slightly smaller — about 39 in (100 mm) with a tail measurement of 32 in (820 mm), but her body weight is considerably less than that of the male — seldom more than 60 pounds (26.5 kg).

The Red Kangaroos have adapted to the long, dry periods and sudden rains of their open plains habitat. They usually stay in one area but have been known to move 120 miles (193 km) in times of drought.

Potoroos are found in densely growing grasses and tussocks in forests and woodlands.

Their small size makes them seek the protection of the dense vegetation against birds of prey, reptiles and other carnivorous animals. They are strictly nocturnal.

Potoroos appear to be quite long lived for small animals. They may live for as long as seven years in the wild.

The Parma Wallaby lives in wet forest areas with a thick shrub coverage, where it can shelter during the day, emerging at night to feed on grasses and herbs.

When it hops, it keeps its body close to the ground, almost horizontal, with its forepaws tucked up against its body.

It was thought to be extinct, but in 1967 it was found to be surviving on the eastern coast of northern New South Wales.

The word Pademelon is a corruption of a roughly similar aboriginal word for the smaller wallabies found on the east coast of Australia, from Tasmania up to Cape York in Queensland.

As well as eating grass, these small creatures dig up roots and small plants and sit back on their haunches to eat them, holding them very daintily in their forepaws.

Tree Kangaroos are believed to have developed in New Guinea and entered Australia when a land bridge connected the two countries. Their ancestors were small possum-like creatures which made the most of their kangaroo-like features.

Their heavy tails lengthened and strengthened so that they could be used as supple pendulums or as balancing poles. Their long hind legs became shorter and their short forelegs lengthened. In their evolution, the teeth of the Tree Kangaroo have changed from those required for nibbling and adapted to leaf browsing and fruit eating.

The pads of their feet are soft and hairy which helps them grip branches when they land after one of their incredible leaps from tree to tree. Although they are essentially tree dwellers, they spend some time on the ground, but, if disturbed, will climb back into the trees.

Although the Bennett's Wallaby's thick fur is white or pale grey when young, it darkens to grey brown when full grown.

It subsists on grasses and herbs and has benefited from clearing for stock grazing by farmers, where some patches of forest have been left on hill tops or along creeks, providing shelter.

This wallaby was named after a distinguished medical man and naturalist, Dr. George Bennett, who was one of the founders of the Australian Museum.

The young kangaroo in the pouch is called a 'joey'. The Oxford Dictionary defines a 'joey' as a 'young kangaroo' and although it is not a scientific term, it is widely used and accepted.

The Rock Wallaby can leap with cat-like precision from ledge to ledge. The thick pads on its feet help it to grip rocky surfaces and its long hairy tail acts as a balance.

On level ground, the Rock Wallaby travels with its head held low and its tail arched upwards, to keep it clear of the ground. It looks somewhat awkward, but it is a different creature when it is leaping over rocky outcrops and huge boulders.

It comes out of its rocky shelter in the late afternoon or evening.

Most four-legged animals have the same sort of rectangular body, with its shape and weight evenly distributed over the four legs.

But the kangaroo is different. Its body is more of a triangle with its small head and chest tapering down to a large stomach and hip area.

Its weight is supported by the very powerful tail. Its front legs take only some of the weight when the animal is grazing or moving slowly.

A kangaroo cannot walk in the normal way, nor can it easily move backwards.

The tail serves mainly as a counter-weight to the top part of the body and allows the animal to sit comfortably in a squatting position, with the large feet in front and the strong tail behind.

Many theories have been advanced to explain why the kangaroo developed its hopping method of propulsion.

One theory is that it was the best method of covering rough ground. Another is that its rapid leaping and zig-zagging helped it escape from its enemies.

Or it could be that its ability to sustain high speeds for long periods enabled it to survive.

When a kangaroo is moving quickly, the front paws are tucked under the chest or they dangle there with the paws crossed over.

The massive tendons and ligaments which run through the rear legs and tail supply the energy which is released when the feet are about to leave the ground. This gives the legs the extra thrust which enables the animal to cover the ground in gigantic leaps.

The kangaroo can land on uneven surfaces without stumbling and, if suddenly faced with large obstacles, such as rocks or trees, it will merely leap over them or change direction without stopping.

It can run at about 40 miles an hour (60-70 km) but, after about two miles at this speed, it will begin to tire.

The size of groups varies considerably with the territories of each type.

A group might consist of a dominant male, a number of adult females and a few juveniles of both sexes, but some groups can be as small as two or three, or as large as several hundred.

Small groups of young males are often found, but old scarred males may live the rest of their lives as solitary individuals.

On the open grassland, where hiding from predators is not easy, flight is the best means of escape and the larger the group is, the more eyes there are to detect danger.

Male kangaroos fight to keep their territory. The dominant male in the group will fight outsiders who want to mate with the females in his 'harem'.

The bucks attack with their forepaws, scratching with their razor-sharp claws but keeping their heads thrown back to avoid damage to their eyes.

They also attack with their hind feet, with strong claws sharp enough to tear into their opponent's belly. The weight of the whole body is taken by the strong tail.

Most fighting is reserved for battles of dominance between males, but if attacked by dogs or dingoes, a big buck is more than a match for its attacker. In its natural habitat, the kangaroo never attacks unless provoked.

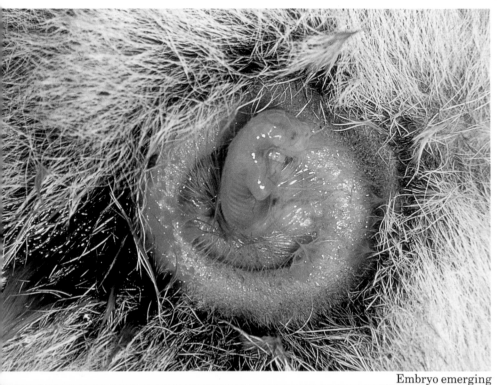

Embryo emerging

2 days

The birth of the young marsupial takes places after a gestation period of thirty to forty days.

The doe moves away from the group and sits with her tail and her hind legs extended in front of her. She licks the inside of the fold of skin which forms a pouch on her belly.

A few moments later, she gives birth to a barely-formed embryo, a tiny, hairless, blind creature, only three quarters of an inch (2 cm) long. This tiny creature's forearms and claws are developed enough to enable it to haul itself up through the fur on its mother's belly and into her pouch.

This takes about three minutes, but it is a mammoth journey for this tiny blind creature, which weighs only a fraction of an ounce (.5 gram). It is not certain what guides the embryo through the fur to find the pouch, but it is an incredible feat when you consider that it receives no help from the mother.

Once it reaches the lip of the pouch, it is probably scent which guides the embryo on to one of the four teats in the pouch.

20

When the embryo clamps its mouth on to a teat, it swells until it almost fills the mouth. This prevents it being dislodged if the mother has to move off quickly.

Because of its small size, the embryo's need for milk is very low and its sucking is weak. For the first three months it grows and develops very slowly.

A pronounced growth phase begins at about 15 weeks, with the milk supply increasing and its composition changing to meet the needs of the growing young one. The fat and protein content increases and the sugar content is reduced as the baby grows.

The film which covered its eyes and ears has now gone, although the eyes are not yet open.

Its claws are now quite long and its tail well defined.

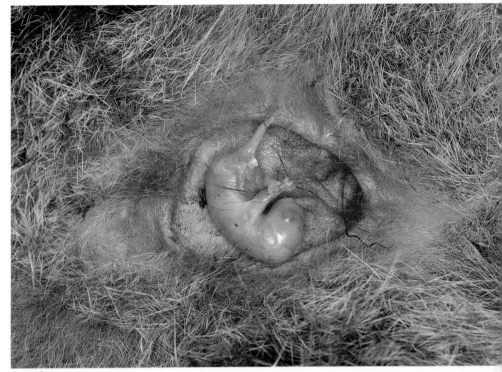
3 weeks

12 weeks

At seventeen weeks, the eyes are now open but, although the film no longer covers the ears, they are still folded back.

The claws are very well developed, particularly those on the hindfeet, but, at this stage, the joey is still hairless.

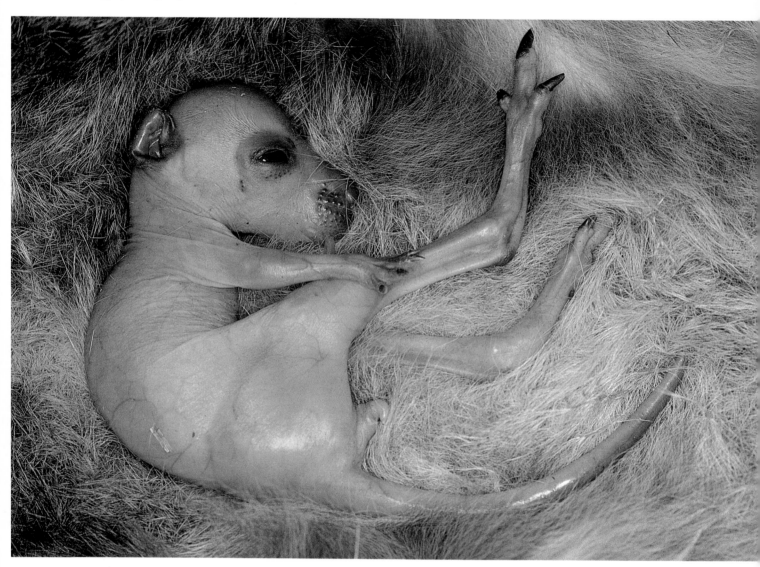

About six months after birth the young joey's fur has grown and its system is able to regulate its own temperature. The mother's milk changes to high fat content and low carbohydrate.

By the time it is nine months old it is ready to leave the pouch for short spells, but the mother will not let it out until she has checked the surroundings for danger.

In the next few months, the young kangaroo will spend more time out of the pouch than in it, but it will continue to return to the mother for an occasional drink. Its diet becomes a blend of milk and grass.

Gradually the periods inside the pouch become shorter, until finally it is wholly independent. By this time it has become too large for the pouch but it is well enough developed to be able to keep up with the mother if she has to flee from danger.

She will warn her young with a quick stamp of her hindfeet. This also acts as an alarm for the rest of the group.

Although independent, the joey will continue to take milk from its mother from outside the pouch until it is about one year old.

This mother suddenly became aware of the photographer and gave her baby a warning to get back into the security of the pouch.

The does will graze together, moving gently about on all fours.

At the slightest noise, they will spring upright on their hind legs, listening and assessing the potential danger.

If the noise persists, the female will often 'bounce' the joey out of her pouch. Whether this is intentional or not, it obviously improves the chances of survival for both mother and joey.

Eagles or dingoes used to be the main predators of the young kangaroo, but today more kangaroos are pursued by hunters in 4-wheel drive vehicles.

While an albino is not rare in the marsupial world, it is very uncommon — perhaps one in about 10,000 births.

The mating of this albino Red-necked Wallaby with a male of a pure strain had produced a normal joey.

Had she mated with an albino male, the chances of the young wallaby being an albino also would have been much greater.

When the weather is extremely
hot, the kangaroo will dig
away the top soil . . .

and flop down in the cooler
soil of the hollow . . .

and sleep!

On the hot dry plains, kangaroos keep cool by licking their forearms which have very little hair on them and where the blood vessels are close to the surface.

When this moisture evaporates, excess body heat evaporates with it, helping the cooling process.

On mild days, they like to bask in the sun.

This joey is enjoying the warm sun, but won't leave the security of its mother's pouch.

Some grazing wallabies, which live largely on grasses and herbs, enjoy eating bark from wattle, eucalypt and paper-bark trees.

This night shot shows a King Island Red-necked Wallaby eating a strip of bark. If there are succulent leaves and small branches attached to the bark, sometimes they too will be eaten.

This obviously adds some variety to their normal diet but, in addition, it toughens their teeth and cleans and hardens the gums.

The King Island Red-necked Wallaby is common in the forests of south eastern Australia, including Tasmania and the islands in Bass Strait, which separates the state of Tasmania from the mainland.

King Island, after which this wallaby is named, is one of these islands.

Although frequently seen drinking at stock watering places, many species appear to be able to exist without access to fresh surface water, providing there is some green herbage. But when water is available, it is appreciated. Some large kangaroos have been seen drinking without pause for nearly two minutes.

Some wallabies are able to obtain fresh water from the salty juice of succulent plants. Some, like the Tammar Wallaby, are able to drink sea water.

The kangaroo is a very strong swimmer but it will take to the water only when it is pursued and has no other refuge, such as in a bush fire. Although a kangaroo cannot walk in the normal way, it kicks its hind legs alternately when swimming.

Between the tropical north of Australia and the much colder regions of the south there is a wide variety of land masses and climates.

Different species of kangaroos and wallabies survive equally as well in the savannahs and grasslands, the eucalypt woodlands and rocky hill country.

The greatest numbers of this Whiptail Wallaby are found in southern Queensland and northern New South Wales, in undulating or hilly country.

These Grey Kangaroos feed mainly on grasses in forests and woodlands. Their general colour is a soft 'donkey' grey and their fur is longer and coarser than the other well-known grey marsupial — the Koala.

The Grey's elegant ears are so flexible that they can be turned round to catch the sound of an enemy approaching from any direction.

When sheep were introduced into Australia and allowed to run in open pastures, this may have made the environment even more suitable for the Red Kangaroo than it was previously. The woodlands changed to grasslands and allowed the kangaroo population to expand.

Many farmers complain that kangaroos are competing with their stock and their numbers must be reduced but, weight for weight, kangaroos do not eat more than sheep and, in good years, scarcely compete with them.

In bad years, shortages of grass and other plants may cause sheep and kangaroos to compete with each other, but the kangaroo population is mostly on land that is only marginally suitable for agriculture.

Man will probably continue to encroach on the natural habitat of the animals which were on the land long before he arrived in Australia, but, as the kangaroo has survived the most extreme conditions in Australia to date, no doubt it will continue to adjust to any great changes in its habitat which man may bring about.